Dinosaurs and Other First Animals

Words by Dean Morris

Raintree Childrens Books
Milwaukee

Cover Photo: Royal Ontario Museum

Library of Congress Number: 87-16670

 2 3 4 5 6 7 8 9   92 91 90 89 88

Printed and bound in the United States of America

Library of Congress Cataloging in Publication Data

Morris, Dean.
    Dinosaurs and other first animals..

    Includes index.
    Bibliography: p. 47
    Summary: An easy-to-read survey of various
prehistoric animals, emphasizing their relationship
to present-day species.
    1. Dinosaurs—Juvenile literature. 2. Vertebrates,
Fossil—Juvenile literature. [1. Dinosaurs. 2. Prehistoric
animals. 3. Evolution] I. Title.
QE862.D5M65 1987   567.9′1   87-16670
ISBN 0-8172-3206-0 (lib. bdg.)
ISBN 0-8172-3231-1 (softcover)

This book has been reviewed
for accuracy by

Dr. Ted M. Cavender
Curator of Fishes
The Ohio State University Museum of Zoology

Dinosaurs and
Other First Animals

When the earth began, there was nothing but hot gases. Slowly the gases cooled and became rock. Rain fell. Water mixed with salts from the rocks. The first life grew in this mixture.

The first life was in the sea. Tiny plants formed. For millions of years, the plants slowly grew and changed.

Millions of years later, other plants and animals grew. Here you can see some of the animals that lived on the earth long ago.

mammoth

duck-billed
dinosaur

Drepanaspis

Lituites

Prehistoric animals lived on the earth long before there were people to write about them. We know they were here because we still find their remains buried in rock.

Remains of prehistoric animals are called fossils. Scientists who study fossils are called paleontologists. This man is digging a fossil out of a rock.

fossil skeleton

Sometimes paleontologists find the fossil of the whole skeleton of an animal. The skeleton is removed carefully from the rock. The pieces are put together like the skeleton in the picture. Then we can see what the animal looked like.

skeleton of
Iguanodon

Small marine animal fossils are often found in rock. When the animals died, their bodies sank to the mud at the bottom of the sea. Over many years, the mud turned to rock. The shells of the animals formed part of the rock.

fossil of
ammonite shell

These are some marine animals that lived millions of years ago, before there were any land animals.

Some prehistoric sea animals were like animals living today. Jellyfish floated in the water. Worms lived in mud at the bottom of the sea.

This is a trilobite. It lived in the sea millions of years ago, but you won't find trilobites today since they are extinct. An extinct group is one that has died off completely from the earth.

Trilobites lived at the bottom of the sea and found their food in the mud. Feelers helped them find where they were going.

Most trilobites were smaller than your thumb. When a trilobite was disturbed, it curled up into a ball.

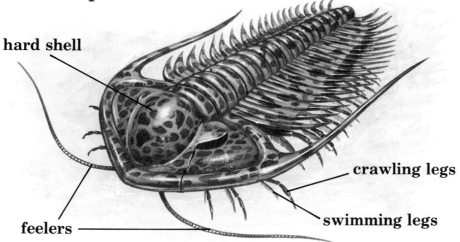

hard shell

feelers

crawling legs

swimming legs

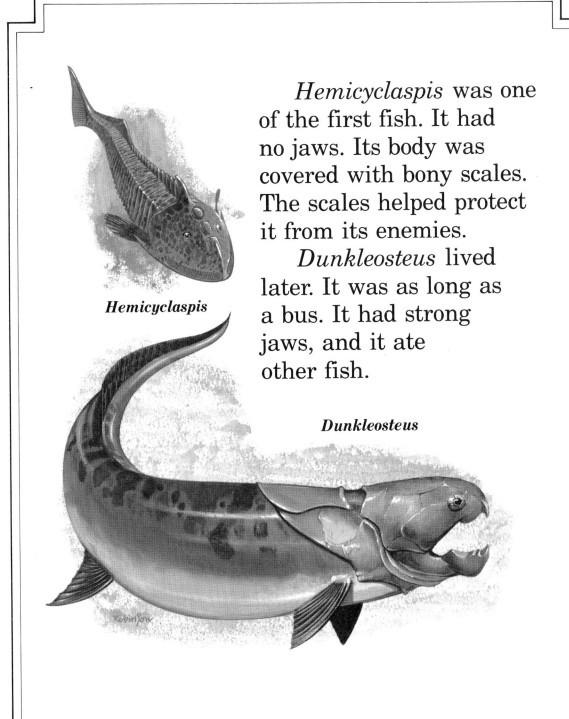

Hemicyclaspis was one of the first fish. It had no jaws. Its body was covered with bony scales. The scales helped protect it from its enemies.

Dunkleosteus lived later. It was as long as a bus. It had strong jaws, and it ate other fish.

Hemicyclaspis

Dunkleosteus

Cladoselache

Cladoselache was one
of the first sharks.
Instead of bone, its
skeleton was cartilage,
like the inside of your
nose. Today's sharks have
skeletons of cartilage too.

Cheirolepis had bones.
An air sac inside its
body helped it to swim.
Many of today's fish
developed from this type
of bony fish.

Cheirolepis

For millions of years, it rained most of the time on earth. But as time passed, less and less rain fell. Rivers and lakes dried up, and many fish died.

At first there were no living things on land. But that changed after a while. Plants, worms, and other small animals began to live on land.

Some fish had lungs and could breathe air. They had strong fins which they could

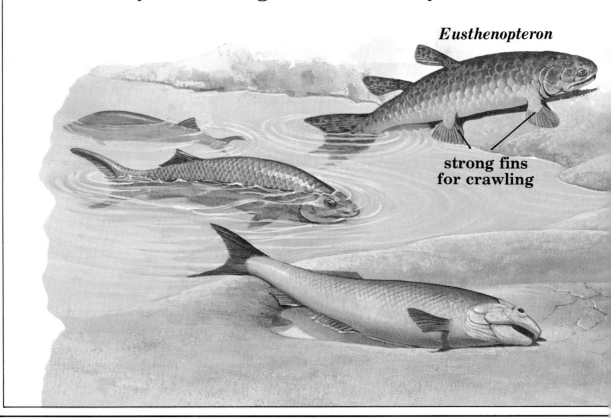

Eusthenopteron

strong fins for crawling

use as legs to walk on the bottom of
lakes and streams. Some left the water for
periods of time and were at home both on the
land and in the water.

Over many years their legs and tails
grew longer and stronger. Their heads
grew bigger. They were the first amphibians.
Amphibians lay their eggs in water but can
also live on land. Like fish, amphibians
are cold-blooded.

early amphibian

Eryops

Some of the first amphibians were very big. *Eryops* was as big as a small crocodile. Its legs were very short. It could not move very fast.

It could not run away from danger. But it had very strong jaws for fighting.

strong jaws

skeleton of *Eryops*

This early amphibian, called *Amphibamus*, looked a little like one of today's salamanders. It was very small.

Amphibamus

The largest amphibian, called *Pteroplax*, was bigger than a crocodile.

Most amphibians lay their eggs in water. The eggs hatch into larvae which stay in water until they are big enough to change into adults and live on land. *Pteroplax* was a water-dwelling amphibian. It did not live on land.

Pteroplax

After millions of years, a new kind of animal appeared on earth. These were the first reptiles. The first reptiles were different from amphibians. Reptiles had scales. They could live on land all the time. Their eggs had thick shells. Reptiles did not have to lay their eggs in water. This was important because they were free to live almost anywhere on land. The amphibian's water home could dry up.

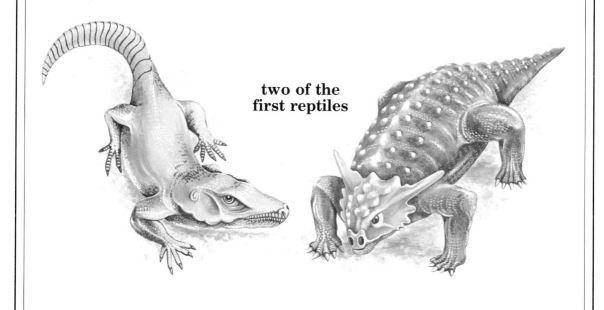

two of the first reptiles

This reptile is called *Dimetrodon*. It had a big fin on its back. The fin helped it to stay warm. The fin had many blood vessels. The sun warmed the blood in the fin, and that blood traveled to the rest of the body. *Dimetrodon* was a meat-eater. It ate small reptiles.

Dimetrodon

These two prehistoric reptiles looked like animals of today.

Proganochelys was one of the first turtles. It had a thick shell.

Mystriosuchus looked like a crocodile. Its mouth was long and pointed.

Proganochelys

Mystriosuchus

This reptile must have lived in trees.
It had wings made of skin and bone.
The reptile used its wings to help it
glide from tree to tree or down to
the ground.

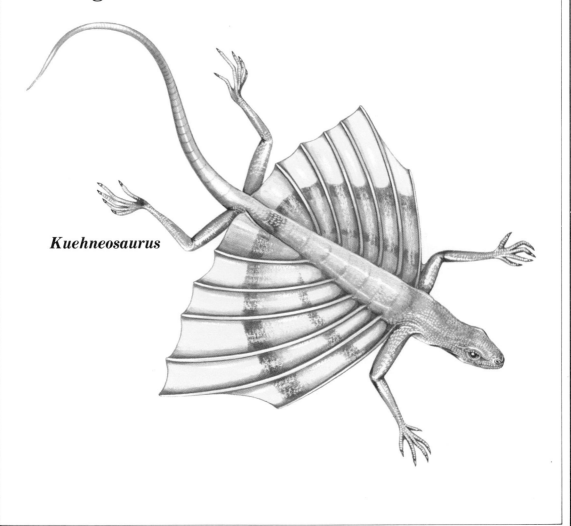

Kuehneosaurus

The biggest reptiles were the dinosaurs. This one, like some others, ate plants. Its spiked tail and the bony plates on its back protected it from enemies.

Some scientists now think that dinosaurs were warm-blooded animals. But this has not been proved.

Stegosaurus

This dinosaur was one of the biggest plant-eaters. It probably used its long neck to reach tree leaves. It was so big that it was safe from most other animals. But its size did not keep it safe from hunger. It must have had to eat all day long to get enough food.

Brontosaurus

The biggest meat-eater was *Tyrannosaurus*. This dinosaur grew to a size more than 36 feet long! It had strong jaws and sharp teeth so it could kill and eat other animals.

Triceratops had a strong, bony plate over its neck. It also had horns. The plate and horns protected it from *Tyrannosaurus* and other enemies.

Triceratops

Tyrannosaurus

Not all reptiles lived on land. Some lived in the sea. One of these, *Ichthyosaurus*, looked like a dolphin and ate small fish.

Plesiosaurus also lived in the sea. Instead of legs, it had flippers. Like some of the dinosaurs, it had a long neck and sharp teeth.

Some reptiles could fly. One, *Pteranodon*, had large wings. The wings measured about eight feet across. *Pteranodon* did not flap its wings. It used them to soar like a glider. It used its bill to catch fish.

Until the 1980s it was thought that *Pteranodon* was the largest flying animal. An animal called *Pterosaur* was found in the United States. It had wings that measured about fifteen feet across.

Pteranodon

Ichthyosaurus

Plesiosaurus

The first bird looked something like
a flying reptile. It lived at the time of
the dinosaurs. It was called *Archaeopteryx*.

Archaeopteryx

We can tell from fossils that *Archaeopteryx* had feathers. It was about the size of a crow.

We do not think it could fly very well. This fossil shows that the bones needed to help move the wings were not very strong. Can you see the bones in the long tail?

Hooked claws at the ends of its wings could have helped it move about in the trees.

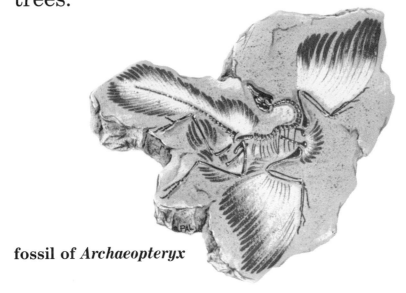

fossil of *Archaeopteryx*

human

Megatherium

Mammals are warm-blooded. Instead of laying eggs, they have live babies. People are mammals.

The first mammals lived at the time of the dinosaurs. They were small and looked something like rats. They may have eaten eggs, lizards, and insects.

Later, after all the dinosaurs died out, or became extinct, the mammals changed. Some grew very large. There were pigs as big as donkeys. Some sloths grew as tall as some trees.

Mammals that have changed a lot are found in the horse family. The first horse was the size of a small dog. It had four toes on its front feet and three on its back feet.

Eohippus

toes

Millions of years later, some horses had three toes on each foot.

Horses today have only one toe on each foot. That is the horse's hoof. Today's horses are a lot bigger than prehistoric horses.

Merychippus

toes

horse

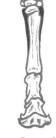

toe or hoof

In the earth's long history there were times when many parts of the earth were covered with ice. We call these very cold times ice ages.

Some ice-age animals, like this mammoth, had thick coats to keep them warm. Animals with less hair probably stayed in warmer parts of the world.

People have found the bodies of mammoths frozen in ice since the last ice age. This helps us know just what the animals looked like.

The last mammoths died about 10,000 years ago. But other ice-age animals—such as foxes, reindeer, and hyenas—are still around.

This big cat lived at the end of the last ice age. Cats like this, with their sharp teeth, hunted other animals in what is now North and South America. Sometimes they might have hunted people.

Smilodon

The first people like us lived during the last ice age. They are known from the stone tools they left behind. They were smaller than many other animals. They were not as strong or as fast. But they were smarter. They learned to use fire to keep other animals away and to cook their food. They made weapons to hunt other animals and wore clothes to keep warm.

People live differently from other animals. But, like all other living things on earth, people are always growing and changing.

Neanderthal Man

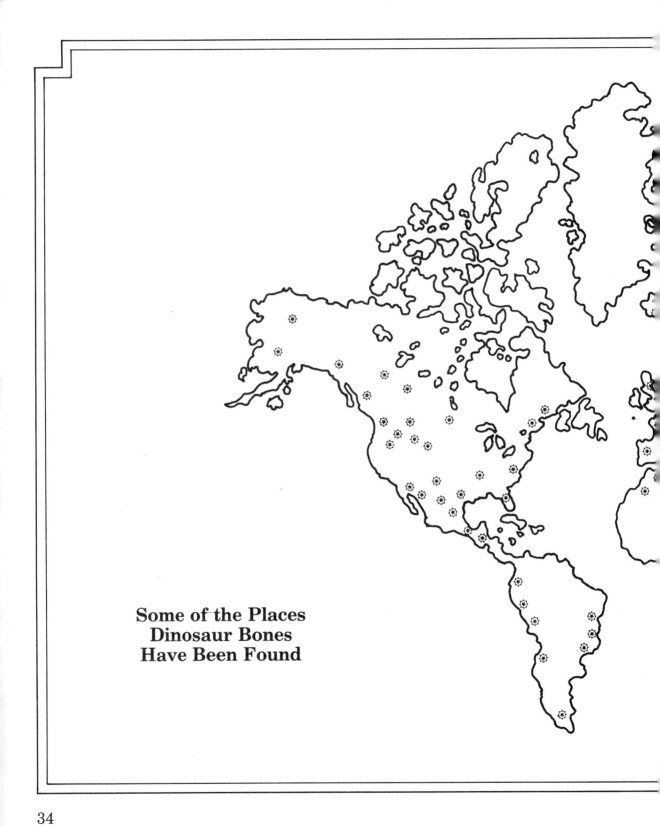

**Some of the Places
Dinosaur Bones
Have Been Found**

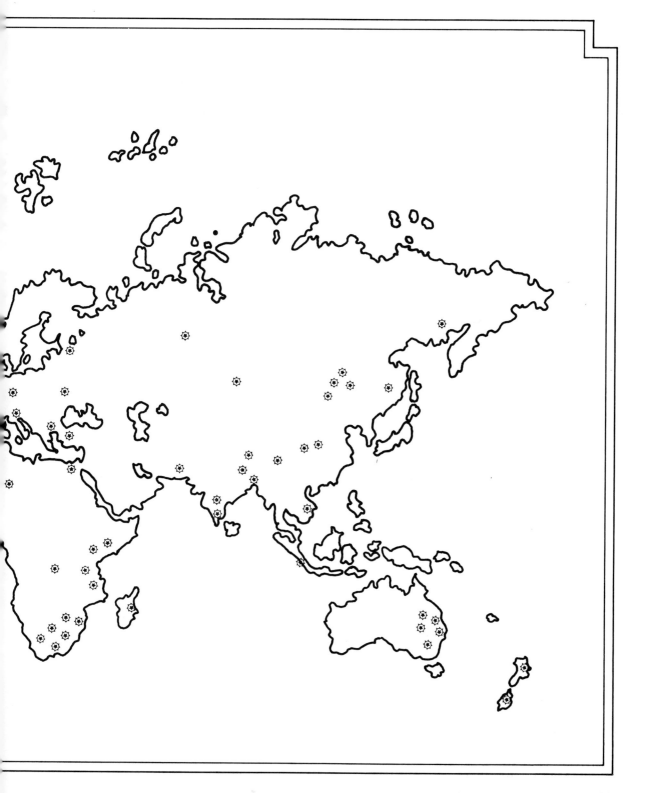

35

Where to Read About the Dinosaurs and Other First Animals

Megatherium (meg′ ə thir′ ē ən) *p. 28*
Merychippus (mer′ ē kip′ əs) *p. 29*
Mystriosuchus (mis′ trē ō sook′ əs) *p. 18*
Neanderthal Man (nē an′ dər thôl′ man) *p. 33*
Plesiosaurus (plē′ sē ō sôr′ əs) *pp. 24, 25*
Proganochelys (prō gan′ ə kēl′ əs) *p.18*
Pteranodon (tə ran′ ə don) *pp. 24, 25*
Pteroplax (tə′ rō plaks) *p. 15*
saber-toothed cat (sā′ bər tootht′ kat) *p. 32*
sloth (slôth *or* slōth) *p. 28*
Smilodon (smī′ lə don) *p. 32*
Stegosaurus (steg′ ə sôr′ əs) *p. 20*
Triceratops (trī ser′ ə tops′) *p. 22*
trilobite (trī′ lə bīt′) *pp. 8, 9*
Tyrannosaurus (tə ran′ ə sôr′ əs) *pp. 22, 23*

Pronunciation Key for Glossary

a	a as in **cat**, **bad**
ā	a as in **able**, ai as in **train**, ay as in **play**
ä	a as in **father**, **car**
e	e as in **bend**, **yet**
ē	e as in **me**, ee as in **feel**, ea as in **beat**, ie as in **piece**, y as in **heavy**
i	i as in **in**, **pig**
ī	i as in **ice**, **time**, ie as in **tie**, y as in **my**
o	o as in **top**
ō	o as in **old**, oa as in **goat**, ow as in **slow**, oe as in **toe**
ô	o as in **cloth**, au as in **caught**, aw as in **paw**, a as in **all**
oo	oo as in **good**, u as in **put**
o͞o	oo as in **tool**, ue as in **blue**
oi	oi as in **oil**, oy as in **toy**
ou	ou as in **out**, ow as in **plow**
u	u as in **up**, **gun**, o as in **other**
ur	ur as in **fur**, er as in **person**, ir as in **bird**, or as in **work**
yoo	u as in **use**, ew as in **few**
ə	a as in **again**, e as in **broken**, i as in **pencil**, o as in **attention**, u as in **surprise**
ch	ch as in **such**
ng	ng as in **sing**
sh	sh as in **shell**, **wish**
th	th as in **three**, **bath**
<u>th</u>	th as in **that**, **together**

GLOSSARY

These words are defined the way they are used in this book.

amphibian (əm fib′ ē ən) a cold-blooded animal with a backbone that lives both on land and in the water

adult (ədult′ *or* ad′ult) a person, plant, or animal that is grown up; fully grown

anywhere (en′ ē hwer′) in any place

baby (bā′ bē) a very young person or animal

bill (bil) the hard parts of a bird's mouth

body (bod′ ē) the whole of an animal or plant

bone (bōn) a hard, stiff part of the skeleton of an animal with a backbone

bony (bōn′ ē) having bones; see **bone**

breathe (brēth) to take air into the lungs and send it back out

buried (ber′ēd) covered with earth or rock

cartilage (kärt′əl ij) a strong body
material, softer than bone, like the inside
of your nose

claw (klô) a sharp, curved nail on an
animal's foot

cold-blooded (kōld′ blud′ ed) an animal
that has a body temperature that changes
with the air or water around it

complete (kəm plēt′) whole; all of
something

crocodile (krok′ ə dil′) an animal with
long, strong jaws and tail, short legs, and
scaly skin

crow (krō) a large, black bird

develop (di vel′ əp) to grow and
change in a natural way

dinosaur (di′ nə sôr′) a big reptile
that lived millions of years ago

disturb (dis turb′) to make uneasy

dolphin (dol′ fin) a sea animal with two
flippers, a back fin, a tail, and a mouth
like a bill

donkey (dong′ kē) an animal that looks
like a small horse but has longer ears

extinct (eks tingkt′) no longer found
alive on earth

extra (eks′ trə) more than usually found
or needed

fin (fin) a part of a fish's body
that sticks out; used to swim and keep
balance in the water

flap (flap) to move up and down

flipper (flip′ ər) a wide, flat limb
on a fish or other animal, used for
swimming or moving along on land

float (flōt) to rest on top of air
or water, or move slowly through it

foot (foot) the end of a person's or
animal's leg on which the person or
animal stands and walks

form (fôrm) to take shape

fossil (fos′ əl) remains of an animal
or plant that lived millions of years ago

free (frē) able to move about

frozen (frō zən) made hard when the air
  around a thing is very cold

gas (gas) matter that is not solid
  or liquid and has no shape

glide (glīd) to float on air

hatch (hach) to come from inside an egg

heat (hēt) warmth

history (his′ tər ē) the record of what
  happened before the present time

hoof (hoof *or* hoof) the hard cover on the
  feet of a horse and some other animals

hooked (hooked) curved

hunger (hung′gər) the feeling a person
  or animal has when the person or animal
  has not had enough to eat

hyena (hī ēn′ ə) an animal that looks
  like a dog or wolf

ice age (īs āj) a period of time when
  most of the earth was covered by ice and
  snow

insect (in′ sekt) a small animal with
  no backbone, such as a fly or ant

jaw (jô) the top or bottom bony mouthpart
of a person or animal

known (nōn) understood as a fact

larva (lär′ və) the wormlike form of
an insect after it hatches from an egg
plural **larvae**

life (līf) something plants and animals
have that lets them grow and develop

lizard (liz′ərd) a four-legged animal
with a long body and tail and scaly skin

lose (lōōz) to have no longer; to be without

lung (lung) one of two organs in an
animal's chest, used for breathing

mammal (mam′ əl) a warm-blooded animal
with a backbone, usually having hair or fur

marine (mər ēn′) living in the ocean; of
the sea

million (mil′ yən) the number 1,000,000

mix (miks) to put some different things
together

mixture (miks′ chər) something made up
of two or more things put together

paleontologist (pā lē on' tol' ə jəst)
a scientist who studies fossils to find
out about life during other periods of time

period (pēr' ē əd) a length of time

plate (plāt) a hard, flat covering
that helps protect an animal

prehistoric (prē' his tôr' ik) something
that lived or happened before people began
to write things down

rat (rat) an animal that looks like a
mouse but is bigger

ray (rā) a beam of light

reindeer (rān' dēr') a large deer with
antlers

remains (ri mānz') a dead body

remove (ri moov') to take or move
something away

reptile (rep'til *or* rep'tīl) a cold-
blooded animal with a backbone and dry,
scaly skin

sac (sak) a bag-shaped part of a plant or
animal which often holds a liquid

salamander (sal′ ə man′ dər) a lizardlike
fresh-water animal

scale (skāl) one of many hard, flat parts
of the outer covering of fish and snakes

scientist (sī′ən tist) someone who has
studied a great deal about a branch of
science

shark (shärk) a kind of fish with very
sharp teeth

sharp (shärp) able to cut something or make
a hole in something easily

skeleton (skel′ ə tən) a frame of bones
in the body of a person or animal

skin (skin) the outer covering of a body

spike (spīk) something with a sharp
point

stream (strēm) water that flows along
in a course

study (stud′ ē) to find out about something
by reading and thinking

toe (tō) one of five parts at the end
of a person's or some animal's feet

tool (to͞ol) something a person uses to do work or to make something

thumb (thum) a finger that is shorter and thicker than the other fingers on a person's hand, used to pick things up

turtle (turt′ əl) an animal with a low, wide body that has a shell covering it

type (tīp) a kind or group of things that are alike in some ways

warm-blooded (wôrm′ blud′ id) having almost the same body temperature all the time

water-dwelling (wô′tər dwel′ing) living in or close to water

weapon (wep′ ən) something that is used for fighting

write (rīt) to put words on paper or other material so they can be read

Bibliography

Dixon, Dougal. *Prehistoric Reptiles.* New York: Gloucester Press, 1984

Eastman, David. *Story of Dinosaurs.* Mahwah, New Jersey: Troll Associates, 1982.

Halstead, Beverly. *Brontosaurus, the Thunder Lizard.* New York: Franklin Watts, 1983.

Oliver, Rupert. *The New Dinosaur Library.* Windermere, Florida: Rourke, 1984.

Selsam, Millicent. *A First Look at Dinosaurs.* New York: Walker, 1982.

Wilson, Ron. *Pteranodon.* Windermere, Florida: Rourke, 1984.